The Missions of California

Mission La Purísima Concepción

Kim Ostrow

The Rosen Publishing Group's
PowerKids Press™
New York

For RK—my favorite mission.

Published in 2000, 2003 by The Rosen Publishing Group, Inc.
29 East 21st Street, New York, NY 10010

Photo Credits and Photo Illustrations: pp.1, 5, 13, 20, 23, 24, 26, 30, 31, 32, 33, 35, 36, 37, 38, 43, 48, 49 by Cristina Taccone; pp. 4, 17, 27, 51, 57 by Shirley Jordan; p. 6 Courtesy of National Park Service, Cabrillo National Monument; pp. 9, 16 Seaver Center for Western History Research, Los Angeles County Museum of Natural History; pp. 10, 45 © The Granger Collection, New York; pp. 14, 15, 18, 21, 41 by Michael K. Ward; p. 25 The Bancroft Library; p. 29 Courtesy of Mission La Purísima Concepción; p. 46 Santa Bárbara Mission Archive – Library; p. 51 by Christine Innamorato.

Revised Edition 2003

Book Design: Danielle Primiceri

Layout: Michael de Guzman

Editorial Consultant Coordinator: Karen Fontanetta, M.A., Curator, Mission San Miguel Arcángel
Editorial Consultant: Dr. Robert L. Hoover, California Historical Resources Commission
Historical Photo Consultants: Thomas L. Davis, M. Div., M.A.
Michael K. Ward, M.A.

Ostrow, Kim.
    Mission La Purísima Concepción / by Kim Ostrow.
    p. cm. — (The missions of California)
    Summary: The history of this California mission from its founding in 1787, through its development and use in serving the Chumash Indians and its secularization and function today.
    ISBN 0-8239-5881-7 (lib. bdg.)
    1. Mission La Purísima Concepción (Calif.)—History—Juvenile literature. 2. Spanish mission buildings—California—Lompoc Region—History—Juvenile literature. 3. Franciscans—California—Lompoc Region—History —Juvenile literature. 4. Chumash Indians—Missions—California—Lompoc Region—History—Juvenile literature. 5. California—History—To 1846—Juvenile literature. [1. Mission La Purísima Concepción (Calif.)—History. 2. Missions—California. 3. Chumash Indians—Missions—California. 4. California—History—To 1846. 5. Indians of North America—Missions—California.] I. Title. II. Series.
F869.M65 078 1999
979.4'91—dc21   99-19531
                                                                   CIP

Manufactured in the United States of America

Contents

Exploration in California

Along the beautiful California highway known as El Camino Real stand the 21 missions that helped shape California's rich and fascinating history.

In 1769, the first mission, Mission San Diego de Alcalá, was built. It was to be a place where Catholic friars from Spain could teach their religion to the California Indians. The purpose of each of the 21 missions was the same, to spread the Spanish culture and religion. However, each mission has its own incredible story of how it began and developed and how it helped shape the history of California. Mission La Purísima Concepción, the 11th mission founded, has survived earthquakes and political rebellions. Its historic walls tell a story of strong beliefs, hard work, and incredible loss of life.

Juan Rodríguez Cabrillo

For thousands of years before California was part of the United States, the rich desert and mountainous land were home to many American Indian groups. The Hupa, Pomo, Yuma, and Chumash were some of the groups

The Royal Road, El Camino Real, is now a historical landmark in California.

This is a view of the church at Mission La Purísima Concepción as it looks today. ▶

4

Spanish explorer Juan Rodríguez Cabrillo ▶

living throughout the western region of North America.

In 1541, Antonio de Mendoza, the viceroy of New Spain, realized there was a whole world to be explored. Today New Spain is the country of Mexico. Mendoza told a sailor named Juan Rodríguez Cabrillo to set out and explore the Pacific Coast. In 1542, Cabrillo sailed away with three ships, the *San Salvador*, the *Victoria*, and the *San Miguel*. He began his trip on June 27, 1542, from a city called Navidad, which is known today as Acapulco, and headed along the Pacific Coast. The king of Spain wanted him to find a shorter route from the Pacific Coast to Spain. At that time, many people thought there was a river running across America that connected the Atlantic and Pacific Oceans. If such a river were found, it would mean that Spanish ships could easily bring back gold, silk, dyes, spices, tea, and other treasures from Asia.

Cabrillo and his crew were also supposed to locate harbors where Spanish ships could dock during long trips.

The first port that Cabrillo and his crew found was the San Diego Bay. They stayed there for a while before continuing on their journey. This area would later become the site for the first California mission, Mission San Diego de Alcalá. As they continued their trip heading north, Cabrillo and his crew met many Indians from different villages. These Indians welcomed Cabrillo and his men, and gave them fish and other goods that they could use in their travels.

With winter on its way, Cabrillo needed to find a safe place for his crew. He chose San Miguel Island, in the Santa Barbara Channel, for himself and his crew to settle on. Some sources say that Cabrillo died on this island. Others believe that Cabrillo and his crew traveled farther south to the island now known as

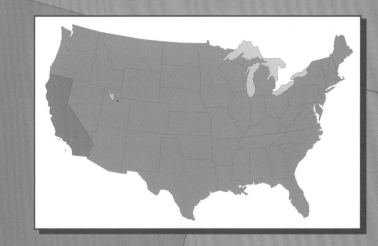

San Francisco Solano

San Rafael Arcángel

San Francisco de Asís

San José

Santa Clara de Asís

Santa Cruz

San Juan Bautista

San Carlos Borromeo de Carmelo

Nuestra Señora de la Soledad

San Antonio de Padua

San Miguel Arcángel

San Luis Obispo de Tolosa

La Purísima Concepción

Santa Inés

Santa Bárbara

San Buenaventura

San Fernando Rey de España

San Gabriel Arcángel

San Juan Capistrano

San Luis Rey de Francia

San Diego de Alcalá

Santa Catalina. No one knows for sure upon which island Cabrillo died. To this day, he is remembered as the first European to explore the California coast. According to Cabrillo's wishes, his crew continued the journey after his death. When the remaining crew returned home to New Spain, they had not fulfilled any of the king's wishes. However, they were able to pass on valuable information to future explorers.

Sebastián Vizcaíno

Spain sent an explorer named Sebastián Vizcaíno to look for a river that connected the Pacific and Atlantic Oceans, and to find a good harbor in Alta, or upper, California. Vizcaíno was an experienced sailor and had led many other expeditions in the areas now known as Mexico and Guatemala. He set sail for the California coast in 1602. He visited many places along the coast, including Monterey Bay, which he named after the viceroy of New Spain.

Vizcaíno was promised many rewards, including the command of a large ship, if he found a good harbor. Vizcaíno was afraid he would not get all he was promised if he didn't send home excellent reports about California. He told Spain's rulers that there was an excellent harbor in Monterey Bay. The viceroy of New Spain wanted to set up a port in Monterey, but before this could happen the viceroy was promoted and the plan was abandoned. For the next 160 years, no Spanish ships sailed to California.

Captain Gaspár de Portolá

By the mid-1700s, the English and Russians were exploring the California area. The Russians set up a military fort to protect Russian fur traders. When Spain's rulers heard about these explorations, they feared they would lose their land to another country. To protect its claim to California, Spain chose Gaspár de Portolá as the governor of Alta California. In 1769, Portolá was told to lead an expedition to the California coast. He was urged to establish settlements in Alta California. King Carlos III of Spain wanted to strengthen and expand the Spanish foothold in California. The Spanish government also wanted to convert the Indians already living in California into Catholic Spanish citizens. The government decided to send friars to teach the Indians about Christianity and the Spanish way of life. One of the friars who traveled with Portolá was Fray Junípero Serra. Serra had been chosen as the president of the California missions. This meant that he would found and supervise all of Spain's new missions in Alta California.

The first military governor of Alta California, Gaspár de Portolá, led the expedition to California in 1769.

9

The Beginning of the Mission System

Fray Serra

Miguel José Serra was born on November 24, 1713. He grew up in a small village on the island of Majorca, Spain. After deciding at a young age that he wanted to devote his life to God, at the age of 16 Serra began studying to be a priest. He spent many years at the Convent of San Francisco, located in Palma, the capital of Majorca. In 1737, he became a Franciscan priest. The Franciscans were a communal Roman Catholic order of friars, or "brothers." Most friars were priests. The Franciscans tried to model their lives after a man named Saint Francis of Assisi. Saint Francis of Assisi had done much work as a missionary. Missionary work, or spreading one's religious faith to new places and people, was important to the people who became Saint Francis's followers.

When a man joins the Franciscan order, he also chooses a new name for himself. Serra chose the name Junípero, after one of Saint Francis's most devoted followers. Once he became a priest, Fray Serra taught classes and ran the library at the monastery. *Fray* is the Spanish word for friar. Although Serra was a successful teacher, he also wished to spread his knowledge to people in other countries. He wanted to become a missionary. Christian missionaries believe that everyone should follow the teachings of Jesus Christ and the Bible, so they travel to foreign lands to convert people to Christianity.

◀ *When Miguel José Serra joined the Franciscan order, his name changed to Junípero, after Brother Juniper, friend and companion of Saint Francis of Assisi.*

Missionary Work in the New World

In 1749, Serra finally had the opportunity to become a missionary. In the New World (North America, South America, and Central America) he would be able to spread his love of Christianity to the American Indians who were not familiar with this religion. It would be a long, hard trip, but the Franciscans believed a difficult journey would affirm their belief in God.

Fray Serra's assignment was to go to the towns, villages, and mining camps outside of Mexico City. Serra traveled with two of his former students, Juan Crespí and Francisco Palóu. The journey was long. The temperatures were incredibly hot. Once he arrived in the New World, Serra had to walk over 269 miles (433 km) from Veracruz to Mexico City. As he traveled, he gave sermons about Christianity and tried to convince people to join the Christian faith.

Alta California Missions

In 1768, after working hard to spread Christianity throughout New Spain, Junípero Serra was chosen to become the president of the Alta California missions. He was a natural choice because of the work he had accomplished at the missions of New Spain. On July 16, Serra, now 55, founded the first mission in Alta California, San Diego de Alcalá. Serra was president of the missions for 15 years and founded nine of the 21 Alta California missions. The missions were connected by a long dirt road called El Camino Real, meaning "The Royal Road." Parts of this road are still used today.

In order to start a mission, the friars first had to get permission from the Spanish viceroy. A friar was then sent to find the perfect piece of land. There were many important things to look for when choosing a mission site. First, fresh water was necessary for drinking, bathing, and watering crops. Fertile soil was also needed to grow fruits and vegetables. A large area of land was needed for horses, cattle, sheep, and other livestock. Lastly, a great deal of wood was necessary to make the mission buildings. All of these elements in combination would help to make a successful mission. Finding the best location also included locating an area inhabited by many Indians. This was necessary because the main purpose of the mission was to teach religion and European ways to the Indians and make them Spanish citizens. When the friars found a place with all the conditions they needed, a large cross was built where the church would eventually be constructed. The land would be blessed with a sprinkling of Holy Water. In the Christian religion, water blessed by a priest is thought to be sacred and is used in many religious ceremonies and rituals.

When a mission was founded, the land was blessed by the priests and claimed for God, ▶ *King, and Spain. This was done by raising a large wooden cross.*

The Chumash Indians

Along the coast of California lived an Indian tribe known for their peacefulness. This tribe was called the Chumash. It has been said that the Chumash lived along this coast for thousands of years and that their ancestors date back as far as the Ice Age.

Harmony with Nature

The Chumash Indians used the land they lived on without destroying the environment. They made all of their clothing and food from nature. They believed the land was a gift from their creator and if they respected nature and treated the land with care, it would provide them with everything they needed. The Chumash often had ceremonies to celebrate and honor their land. For example, during the fall harvest, when lots of food was available, the Indians celebrated the plentiful gifts from nature. They had a ceremony where they shared food with their fellow tribespeople and celebrated all that nature had given them. They also had a winter celebration in which they honored the sun and waited excitedly for the return of the warm weather in the springtime.

The Chumash Indians celebrated life through dance, song, and storytelling. ▶

◀ *The Chumash Indians lived in a family-centered village.*

15

The Chumash Indians were great hunters and fishermen. ▶

Music and Crafts

Music and crafts were very special to the Chumash. They had songs for grinding acorns, basketmaking, births, healing, hunting, wars, and the harvest. Sometimes they sang for hours and even days at a stretch! They played instruments such as flutes made from deer bones, rattles made from turtle shells with pebbles inside, and whistles made from the bones of birds. The Chumash did not use drums to keep the beat. Instead they used

clappers made from sticks. The Chumash also loved arts and crafts. They made paints from the earth and used them to color rocks. They also painted their bodies. The Chumash Indians used a lot of red. They made red paint out of a rock called hematite. The Chumash enjoyed making small sculptures out of rocks. They made

◀ *Acorns ground in stone bowls made up a large part of the Chumash diet.*

16

special hats out of feathers for ceremonies. The Chumash did not wear very much clothing. The women wore skirts woven from fibers or made from animal skins. They decorated them with shells and other ornaments. The men wore loincloths made from animal hides if they wore anything at all. Men and women both wore homemade jewelry and body paint.

Travel and Shelter

The Chumash Indians lived in dome-shaped huts. These shelters were made from thatched reeds and poles. Large families shared these

▲

A Chumash home was made from thatched tule, reeds, and poles. Some of the large Chumash homes provided shelter for several families.

▲

The Chumash tomol *was a very well-made boat. They used these boats to fish and travel in the Pacific Ocean.*

houses. These houses could hold as many as 50 people! The Chumash were most famous for the boats they built. They called this kind of boat a *tomol*. *Tomols* are similar to canoes. The boats were between 12 and 24 feet (3.7 m and 7.3 m) long and were often decorated with shells and painted red. These boats were so well made that they could be used on rough ocean waters. The Chumash also traditionally used a *temescal*, or sweathouse. A *temescal* was a building where men in the tribe would go before hunting trips or celebrations. The men would sit around a fire naked. They believed that sweating cleansed their bodies. Afterward the men would bathe in a lake or stream. The *temescal* was also used as a social place and as a place to do work.

Occasionally women used the *temescal* too.

Religion

The Chumash Indians had their own religion before the Spanish friars arrived in California. Much of their religion had to do with their relationship to the natural world. The Chumash had many gods. Myths about Sun and Moon spirits were an important part of religious life. The Chumash also believed in bad spirits. These spirits lived in another world, below the ground. They could come into this world and cause mischief.

Each Chumash village had a shaman, who was a religious leader. The shamans were also medicine men or women who healed the sick and gave wise advice to the members of their tribe.

The Chumash lived happily on their land in harmony with nature for many years. With the arrival of the missionaries, life as they knew it changed forever.

Some of the Chumash converted and stayed at the mission to convert others. Some fled to new lands. Those that continued to live as before were eventually pushed out by new settlers. Since they did not want to convert and did not want to leave, the Spanish treated them poorly. The Chumash Indians revolted and tried to defeat the Spanish, but they lost almost every battle and slowly began to disappear from the land. By 1900, there were fewer than 100 Chumash descendants. The last person who knew how to speak the Chumash language died in 1965.

The Beginning of Mission La Purísima Concepción

Fray Fermín Francisco de Lasuén

On August 28, 1784, Fray Serra died. After 15 years in California, Serra had baptized over 6,000 Indians. Shortly after Serra died, Fray Fermín Francisco de Lasuén was chosen to take his place as president of the California missions. On December 8, 1787, Fray Lasuén named the 11th mission La Purísima Concepción. It was named in honor of Mary, the mother of Jesus Christ. Like Serra, Lasuén believed it was his duty to convert the Indians to Christianity.

Neophytes

An Indian who decided to convert was called a neophyte. Some Chumash did convert, but others were afraid that becoming a neophyte would mean losing their own culture. The Spanish friars also had differing ideas about how to treat the neophytes. At that time, many Europeans thought that the American Indians were

The friars baptized only children who were freely presented by their parents and adults who had been instructed about Christianity and the Spanish way of life.

◀ *The altar in the main church at Mission La Purísima Concepción* not very advanced people. Some friars decided that they should be kind to the Indians and try to help them. Other friars treated the Indians cruelly because they believed that the European way of life was better than that of the Indians. However, the American Indian groups had their own complex and interesting culture. Today we understand that many of the Europeans' actions violated what we consider to be the human rights of the American Indians. All of the California missions tell the story of two cultures that are sometimes in harmony and sometimes in conflict. The history of Mission La Purísima Concepción is no different.

Mission Life

The first few years at La Purísima were very successful. Most neophytes were willing to work as builders and craftsmen at the mission. At first the friars were not strict with the Indians about following mission rules. Except for the busy harvest season, the Chumash were allowed a lot of free time. In their time off, the Chumash would collect seeds and prepare traditional Chumash foods.

Life was becoming more difficult for the Chumash who chose not to join the mission. Spanish settlements were taking over the land. Cattle destroyed the water holes and plants that the Chumash had depended on to survive. The fur of the sea otter had become popular in Asia, and the Spanish government had decided to make a profit off of this luxury item. People from other countries also came to California to hunt the otter illegally. The Chumash Indians found that the trappers disturbed their old ways. This is partially why many Chumash decided to try living at the mission. At least there they would be protected from these people who had little respect for the land and its original inhabitants. By 1804, over 1,520 neophytes lived and worked at La Purísima.

▲

The Chumash Indians were taught to be skilled builders and craftsmen.

The First Site

Building the Mission

Most of the California missions were built the same way. A cross was made out of wood and set into the ground. Next, a temporary church was built and a Mass was held. The missionaries put up the temporary structures so they could pray immediately, then they began to build more permanent buildings. The permanent structures were built to form a four-sided enclosure with a patio in the middle. All of the rooms in the buildings faced the central patio. The placement of these buildings formed a quadrangle and was used because it could be easily protected from outside attacks. The main church acted as one wall of the quadrangle and was usually the first mission structure to be built.

The first permanent church at La Purísima was built in 1789. It was made of adobe bricks. The Indians mixed mud, straw, and water with their bare feet. Then they shaped the mixture into bricks that would bake in the sun. The roof of the church was flat and covered with straw.

Each adobe brick is about 2½ feet (.7 m) long, 1 foot (.30 m) wide, and 8 inches (20.3 cm) thick, and weighs approximately 50 pounds (22.68 kg). ▶

A historical drawing of Mission La Purísima Concepción at its second site ▶

24

The missionaries and Indians used this church for three years until the friars felt that a new and better church was needed. Under the direction of the friars, the mission Indians began building a new church in 1798. There were 920 Indians living at the mission at that time and the church they were using could not hold everyone.

In addition to the church, there were mills for grinding corn, barracks for the soldiers to live in, stores, workshops, and an infirmary. The mission was like a small town. It had everything that the neophytes and friars needed to live. Near the coast there was a *presidio*, or military fort, to protect the missions in the surrounding areas.

▲

Spanish soldiers slept in barracks that looked like this re-creation. Each mission had four soldiers and a corporal assigned to help protect the mission.

This photo shows a portion of the irrigation system at Mission La Purísima Concepción.

Fray Mariano Payeras

In 1804, Fray Mariano Payeras came to La Purísima and made many improvements to life at the mission. Under Payeras's guidance, the mission experienced its greatest success.

The Spanish had introduced new foods to the Indians, such as peas, beans, peaches, olives, and corn. Water supply had been a problem at La Purísima, but Payeras found a way to fix it. Payeras planned an improved irrigation system that brought water from the Santa Inés River to the mission fields. With this advancement, the mission was able to produce more abundant and healthier crops.

Another change that Payeras made was to encourage a positive relationship between the mission and the *pueblos*, or Spanish ranches that were springing up not far from the mission site. The missions and the ranches traded goods such as soap, candles, and wool and leather products. Although the mission was at the peak of its success, there were dangers ahead that even Payeras couldn't prevent.

Disease

The year 1804 brought great material success to La Purísima, but it also brought terrible illness and diseases. The Europeans had already built up immunity to these diseases. The Indians had never been exposed to these diseases before, so their bodies were not prepared. In the three years that followed, one in every three mission Indians died from diseases like measles, mumps, and smallpox. Many Indians were scared by what they saw and ran away from the missions. Payeras tried his best to find those Chumash who ran away. He also tried to lift the spirits of those who stayed at the mission.

Sickness was not the only reason the Chumash fled the mission. There were other problems, too. Mission life was becoming more strict, and many Chumash struggled to follow the rules that covered everything from what the neophytes could eat to the kind of clothes they were allowed to wear. Some neophytes left the mission against the wishes of the friars. Guards were set up to keep the Indians from leaving. Those caught trying to escape were punished by flogging, or whipping. The neophytes could not practice their customs and traditions, and they were basically forced to stay in confinement.

Earthquakes

The year of 1812 was known as "El Año de los Temblores," which means "The Year of the Earthquakes." On December 21, at 10:30 in the morning, a violent earthquake hit La Purísima. The mission shook for four minutes. Buildings crumbled. A few moments later, another earthquake hit the mission, causing serious damage to some of the buildings. When the earth stopped shaking, a severe rainstorm followed. The exposed clay was washed away, destroying whatever structures were left standing. The rains washed out a crack or crevice in the hill behind the mission. Large amounts of mud and sand flowed down around the mission buildings. After the earthquake and the flood, the mission wasn't much more than a few muddy walls rising out of a muddy puddle. The mission Indians thought it was a bad omen, or sign. Many of them refused to stay at the mission site. Fray Payeras decided it would be best to move the mission to a new location.

The earthquakes of 1812 did much damage to the first site of Mission La Purísima Concepción. This historic picture was taken in the late nineteenth century.

The New Site

The friars and the Indians moved to a location four miles (6.4 km) north of the original site and began to rebuild the mission. They chose an area in a canyon called "La Cañada de los Berros," which means "The Canyon of the Watercress." The soil was very rich and fertile. There was a lot of water available from nearby springs, and because the area was sheltered, the winds were never very strong.

Rebuilding

The friars were afraid of another earthquake, so they took special measures when rebuilding. The missionaries decided to build the new mission in a straight line instead of the usual quadrangle shape. La Purísima was the only mission built in a style different from that of the other missions. The friars also planned that the mission walls would be four feet (1.2 m) thick and would have stone columns to reinforce these thick walls. The neophytes finished the main residence building in 1815.

Inside there were rooms for the friars to live in, guestrooms, offices, a store, dining rooms, and a small church.

The friars' working and living quarters were simple.

This model shows the plan for the new site of Mission La Purísima Concepción.

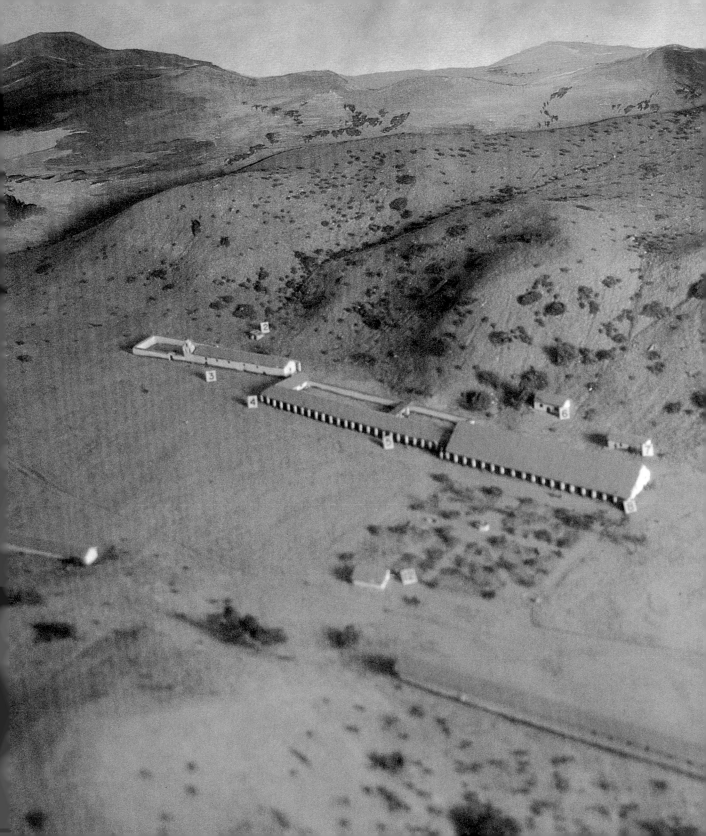

The Chumash enjoyed the church services, which included sacred music. ▶

The Mission Church

The first building to go up in the new location was a church. It was made of temporary materials, but was later replaced by a church made of adobe bricks. The new church was large enough to serve everyone living at La Purísima, including 1,000 American Indians. The church services were held in three languages, Latin, Spanish, and Chumash. Since the Chumash loved music, they were pleased to participate in services that included sacred music. A cemetery was built below the church. Historical records show that hundreds of Indians and Spanish were buried in the cemetery. It became the official church cemetery in 1821. Today the original site of the first cemetery of La Purísima is marked by a small cross.

◀ *A cross marks the site of the cemetery of the second site of La Purísima. This cross is about 10 feet (3 m) high.*

Before the Indians learned how to use gristmills, they had to grind their acorn flour in stone bowls like these.

More Mission Buildings

The gristmill, a machine that grinds corn and wheat to make flour, was located just north of the church. The gristmill was run by a burro. The burro walked in a circle, causing a wheel to turn. Women in the group kitchen used the flour to prepare meals. The group kitchen was where special meals were made for the friars and their guests. The pottery shop was where the Indians created plates, jugs, and thousands

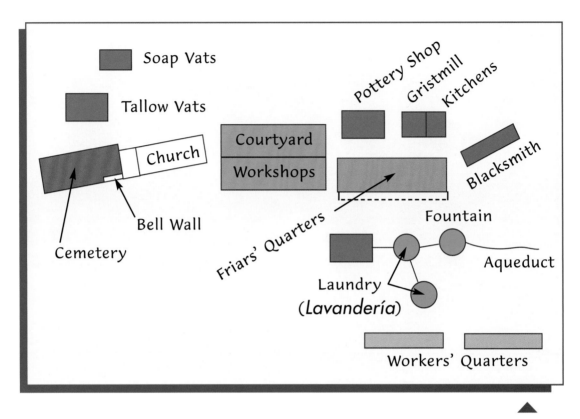

Soap Vats

Tallow Vats

Pottery Shop

Gristmill

Kitchens

Courtyard

Workshops

Church

Blacksmith

Bell Wall

Cemetery

Friars' Quarters

Fountain

Aqueduct

Laundry
(*Lavandería*)

Workers' Quarters

This is the general layout of Mission La Purísima Concepción.

of tiles for floors and roofs. There were other rooms where soap and candles were made, cloth was woven, and leather was tanned. There was also a blacksmith's shop on the mission grounds. The blacksmith made tools out of iron using a machine called a forge.

The springhouse was set a little farther away from the blacksmith's shop and was very important at Mission La Purísima Concepción.

The springhouse was a stone building where the water from the nearby springs was filtered. After being filtered, the water ran underground to the central fountain and other areas of the mission that needed a fresh supply of water. The mission also had a reservoir where it could store water. In 1817, the water system was improved by the addition of another central fountain along with two new washing and rinsing basins.

Housing for the Friars

The fountain at Mission La Purísima Concepción was used for washing clothes.

35

Even the guest rooms for visitors at the mission were simple and plain with little furniture.

The friars lived in the residence building. Inside the residence building were the friars' living area, office space, the mission store, a place for guests, and a church. The friars did not believe in having many luxuries. The rooms were dark and had very little furniture. Their beds were mattresses stuffed with straw. Fleas were a problem for everyone in the mission.

Housing for the Neophytes

The neophytes were housed in separate buildings. Two long adobe buildings served as the Indian dormitories. The Spanish friars believed it was important for young men and women to live apart from each other. The friars wanted the neophytes to follow this rule. Families were separated into girls, boys, unmarried women, single men, and married couples. At some missions, married couples lived in separate housing called *rancherías*. At La Purísima, the living quarters were different. The long buildings were divided into two-room apartments, where married couples lived. The boys and single men slept in the hallways of the mission. The young girls and unmarried women lived slightly farther away in the girls' dormitory called the *monjerío*. The girls were locked in their rooms at night. To be sure they behaved, an older person would watch the girls while they slept. The friars believed that this would help to make them good wives and good Christians. They thought they were protecting the girls from harmful Chumash ideas about marriages, which were different from traditional European marriages. The friars were also worried about Chumash parents teaching their children American Indian traditions.

In the center of the mission garden was a fountain and two reservoirs, one for the mission and one for the Indian barracks. This water was used for many purposes at the mission, such as watering crops or taking baths.

The garden was beautiful. The friars and Indians used plants for many purposes, such as food and medicine. If you walked through the garden at La Purísima, you would find figs, pears, grapevines, and vegetables that the friars and neophytes used.

Just like the housing, there were two infirmaries, one for men and another for women. Unfortunately, as more Europeans settled in California, more diseases came with them. This caused the death rate to continue to rise at all the missions.

This adobe tile reservoir was used to separate soap from the water before the water went to the fields for irrigation. ▶

Daily Life

The Indians were used to waking and sleeping by the position of the sun. They worked when they needed to work. They rested when they needed to rest. The Spanish friars, however, worked on a much stricter schedule. They believed that discipline was an important part of becoming good Christians.

Prayers and Meals

A typical day at La Purísima started early in the morning at 6:00 A.M. A bell tolled and everyone headed to the church to pray. After prayer, breakfast was served. At 7:00 A.M. the workday began. The Chumash men and women went to work and the children stayed behind for religious instruction. The men did leatherworking, woodcraft, and farming. The women's main duty was to prepare the food. They had to learn how to make many Spanish foods. They were also taught how to make candles, soap, and clothing. At noon each day, the Indians ate lunch. They did not eat the acorns or plants they were used to eating. Instead they had either a vegetable or meat stew called *pozole*, or a cornmeal soup called *atole*. After lunch they enjoyed a rest period called a *siesta*. After a *siesta*, everyone worked for a few more hours until 5:00 P.M. when it was time for evening prayers and dinner. The women went to bed at 8:00 P.M. and the men at 9:00 P.M.

The ringing of the mission bells governed daily life for those who lived at the mission. They rang when it was time to wake up, pray, sleep, eat, work, and play.

Indians Revolt

Unfair Treatment

Rough treatment from Spanish and Mexican soldiers has been recorded in many American Indian accounts of mission life. The soldiers' jobs were different from the friars' jobs. They were at the mission to keep order, protect mission life, and punish those who broke mission rules. Some soldiers took advantage of the Indians. If they didn't get their salary from the government, they might take food, clothing, or other goods from the neophytes. Sometimes the soldiers would unjustly whip or flog the neophytes. All of this added to the tension between the Indians and the Spanish.

In 1824, a neophyte from Mission La Purísima visited a relative who was imprisoned at Mission Santa Inés and was whipped by a soldier. The news reached Mission La Purísima very quickly. This made the Indians upset and caused some of them to revolt and take over the mission. Four Mexican travelers were attacked on the road to La Purísima and were killed by the rebelling Indians. Some of the neophytes didn't participate in the revolt. Instead they chose to stay with the imprisoned friars. The mission soldiers barricaded themselves in their living quarters and eventually surrendered. The soldiers were held prisoner while the Mexicans and the neophytes talked. The people were later released, but the fight wasn't over. The Indians controlled Mission La Purísima for almost a month. On March 16, 1824, more Mexican soldiers arrived to suppress the Indian uprising. The soldiers attacked, and the battle lasted only two and a half hours. Sixteen neophytes and one soldier were

This artwork shows Indians revolting against the missions. In 1824, the Chumash revolted against the abuses made upon them by the Mexican soldiers at nearby Mission Santa Inés. ▶

killed. The Indian rebels' weapons were in poor condition compared to those of the soldiers. After the Indians surrendered, seven of them were executed for having killed the Mexican travelers on the first night of the rebellion. Twelve other Indians were sentenced to hard labor for participating in the revolt.

Being defeated by the soldiers was very upsetting to the Indians. Some Indians enjoyed living at the mission. Other neophytes were unhappy with their situation. They resented their lack of freedom and were angry about having to follow strict rules and schedules. It was very difficult for the American Indians to give up their hopes of freedom, but after the revolt many still chose to go back to La Purísima. Some were afraid of what might happen if they did not follow mission life. The longer the Indians spent at the mission, the harder it became to go back to their villages. Returning to their traditional ways was becoming nearly impossible. There was also a new generation of Indians who had been born into the mission system and knew no other way of life.

◀ *This is a photgraph of the cemetery at La Purísima, which is next to the bell tower.*

Secularization

Civil War

In 1821, after years of civil war, New Spain became an independent country and was renamed Mexico. The Mexican government knew that most of the rich and fertile land in California was owned by the missions. Mexico wanted the chance to settle and create a new and prosperous life for its people. The Mexican government wanted to change things and had new plans for the California missions. It wanted to secularize them. This meant that it wanted to make the missions nonreligious. In 1834, this plan was put into action. The land would be given to Mexican settlers. The friars never thought that the California land belonged to them. They had planned to return the land to the Indians once they thought that the Indians were able to live on their own as Spanish citizens. At first the Mexican government promised it would help the Indians and eventually share the mission property with them. This never happened.

Losing the Mission Land

After six months, over half of La Purísima's property had disappeared into the hands of Mexican citizens. The Chumash received only a small portion of the land. The neophytes were split on their feelings about secularization. Many were worried that they could not return to their old way of life. They feared that it would be hard to find safe places to live or that the new generations would not be able to survive using the traditional Chumash ways. Other Indians longed for their old way of life and welcomed the opportunity to be able to return to it.

Many Indians could not make a living off the small pieces of land

Leaders of the Mexican Revolution sought independence from Spain. ▶

they were given and were forced to move away. The old villages that had once belonged to the Chumash were now home to Mexican settlers. The animals that the Chumash had hunted had been pushed off the land by the Spanish's cattle. Some Chumash moved inland, others tried to find work on local ranches or in nearby towns. It was a sad ending for a once prosperous, gentle, and contented Indian tribe.

During the 1930s, the Civilian Conservation Corps began work on restoring Mission La Purísima Concepción.

The missionaries had a dream of settling in California and teaching their ways and religion to the American Indian groups. The friars had good intentions and believed that a new way of life would be the best thing for the neophytes. They did what they believed was right at that time. Today we can see that the rights of the American Indians were not respected and what we consider to be their civil liberties were ignored.

New California Settlers

By 1850, many American settlers had come to California. That same year it became the 31st state of the United States. In 1851, the U.S. government turned Mission La Purísima Concepción back over to the Catholic Church. The mission had changed ownership many times. Thieves stole the beautiful tiles from the mission roof and floor. Bad weather over many years rotted the buildings and churches that had once stood tall and proud. By 1930, La Purísima was in ruin. In 1933, during the Great Depression, a group was formed called the Civilian Conservation Corps. It was created by the American government to help men who were unemployed. A year after its creation, the group was assigned the project of rebuilding and restoring Mission La Purísima Concepción. This project became known as La Purísima Mission State Historical Park. Project workers re-created the mission just as it had appeared in 1820. A piece of California history was brought back to life.

Mission La Purísima
Concepción Today

Today La Purísima Mission State Historical Park is one of only three missions that is a California state park. Everything has been rebuilt to make you feel as if you were back in the 1800s. Project workers planted the garden with the same types of plants that grew in the 1800s, and the mission still has the original aqueduct and water system. If you visit today, you will even see the same types of sheep, goats, and turkeys that lived alongside the Spanish missionaries and the Chumash Indians.

It is possible to take a tour of the mission today. In 1973, volunteers formed a group called "Prelado de los Tesouros," which means "Keeper of the Treasures." These volunteers play the roles of the people who once lived at the mission. You can make candles with them, tour the grounds, or celebrate the founding of the

Today you can see volunteers playing the roles of the people who once lived at Mission La Purísima Concepción.

The mission was turned into a California state park after it was restored.

49

mission at a party called Luminarias. This rich and interesting time in history is brought to life at Mission La Purísima Concepción.

The story of Mission La Purísima Concepción, together with the stories of the other missions, is a critical piece of California's history. California's ethnic heritage is influenced by the intermarriage that took place between Spanish soldiers and American Indians. The locations and populations of many California towns can be traced back to early mission settlements. The mission system is not just a part of California history. It is also a part of U.S. history. Today as we study the way Europeans colonized both the east and west coasts of the United States, we see that great injustice was done to the people already living there. Colonization is no longer an acceptable practice.

The mission system was not intended to destroy the freedoms and culture of California Indians. Indeed the mixing of cultures that came about because of the mission system produced some wonderful cultural and architectural feats, such as the 21 California missions and the many artifacts they still house today. As with many historical events, we must consider the mission system with a critical eye and try to understand both its failures and its successes.

Mission La Purísima Concepción and the other 20 ▶
missions are an important part of California's history.

Make Your Own Model Mission
La Purísima Concepción

To make your own model of Mission La Purísima Concepción, you will need:

foamcore	scissors	glue
green paint	toothpicks	red construction
X-Acto knife	tape	paper
(ask an adult to	pink paint	grass
help)	cardboard	fake flowers

Directions

Step 1: Use a large piece of foamcore that measures 20″ x 30″ (50.8 x 76.2 cm) for the base of your model. Paint the base green and let dry.

20″
(50.8 cm)

30″ (76.2 cm)

Adult supervision is recommended.

Step 2: To make the side walls of the courtyard, cut two pieces of foamcore that measure 16" x 2" (40.6 x 5.1 cm).

16" (40.6 cm)

2" (5.1 cm)

Step 3: To make the end wall of the courtyard, cut a piece of foamcore that measures 5.5" x 2" (14 x 5.1 cm).

2" (5.1 cm)

5.5" (14 cm)

Step 4: To form the courtyard, stick toothpicks into the bottoms of the walls and stick into the foamcore base. Tape the walls at the corners.

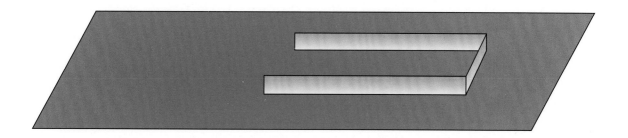

Step 5: To make the church walls, cut out two foamcore pieces that measure 12" x 2.5" (30.5 x 6.4 cm).

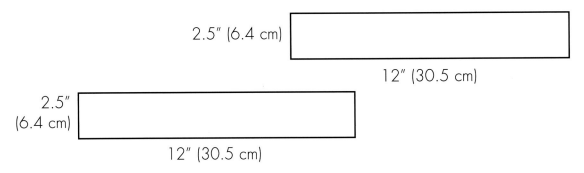

2.5" (6.4 cm)

12" (30.5 cm)

2.5" (6.4 cm)

12" (30.5 cm)

Step 6: Cut two foamcore pieces in the shape of a house, 5.5" x 4.5" (14 x 11.4 cm). The top should be triangular, so it slopes like a roof. The peak of the roof should be off-center.

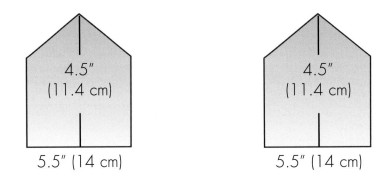

4.5" (11.4 cm)

5.5" (14 cm)

4.5" (11.4 cm)

5.5" (14 cm)

Step 7: Put toothpicks in the bottoms of the church walls and insert into the base. Tape the corners inside the church so the walls stay together.

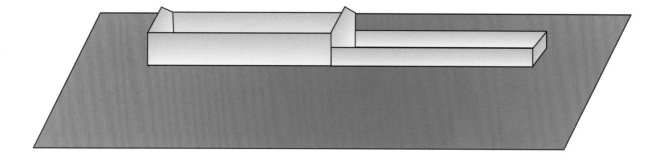

Step 8: Make the bell tower by cutting a piece of foamcore that measures 2.5″ x 5.5″ (6.4 x 14 cm).

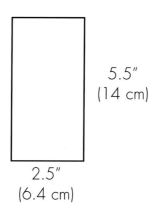

5.5″
(14 cm)

2.5″
(6.4 cm)

Step 9: Cut three bell windows out with an X-Acto knife. Cut the top of the tower in the shape of a dome. With toothpicks, stick the tower onto the base.

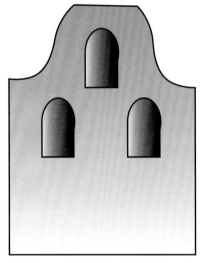

Step 10: Paint the mission walls pink. To make the church roof, cut a piece of cardboard that measures 14" x 3" (35.6 x 7.6 cm). Cut another piece that measures 14" x 4.5" (35.6 x 11.4 cm).

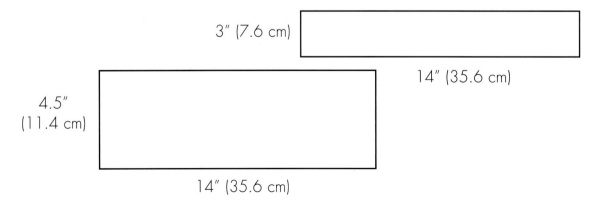

3" (7.6 cm)

14" (35.6 cm)

4.5"
(11.4 cm)

14" (35.6 cm)

Step 11: Glue the cardboard panels on top of the church. Let dry.

Step 12: To make the red tile roof, fold a piece of red construction paper back and forth for a ripple effect. Cut to make it fit both sides of the roof. Glue to the top of the roof.

Step 13: Cut very thin strips of the folded red paper and glue them to the tops of the courtyard walls.

Step 14: Decorate the mission grounds with grass and flowers.

*Use the above mission as a reference for building your mission.

Important Dates in Mission History

1492	Christopher Columbus reaches the West Indies
1542	Cabrillo's expedition to California
1602	Sebastián Vizcaíno sails to California
1713	Fray Junípero Serra is born
1769	Founding of San Diego de Alcalá
1770	Founding of San Carlos Borromeo de Carmelo
1771	Founding of San Antonio de Padua and San Gabriel Arcángel
1772	Founding of San Luis Obispo de Tolosa
1775–76	Founding of San Juan Capistrano
1776	Founding of San Francisco de Asís
1776	Declaration of Independence is signed
1777	Founding of Santa Clara de Asís
1782	Founding of San Buenaventura
1784	Fray Serra dies
1786	Founding of Santa Bárbara
1787	**Founding of La Purísima Concepción**
1791	Founding of Santa Cruz and Nuestra Señora de la Soledad
1797	Founding of San José, San Juan Bautista, San Miguel Arcángel, and San Fernando Rey de España
1798	Founding of San Luis Rey de Francia
1804	Founding of Santa Inés
1817	Founding of San Rafael Arcángel
1823	Founding of San Francisco Solano
1848	Gold found in northern California
1850	California becomes the 31st state

Glossary

adobe (uh-DOH-bee) Sun-dried bricks made of straw, mud, and sometimes manure.

Alta California (AL-tuh kah-luh-FOR-nyuh) The area where the Spanish settled missions, today known as the state of California.

Christian (KRIS-chun) Someone who follows the Christian religion, or the teachings of Jesus Christ and the Bible.

colonization (kah-luh-nuh-ZAY-shun) The settlement of one part of the world by people from another region.

convert (kun-VERT) To change religious beliefs.

Franciscan (fran-SIS-kin) A member of a communal Roman Catholic order of friars, or brothers, who follow the teachings and examples of Saint Francis of Assisi, who did much work as a missionary.

friar (FRY-ur) A brother in a communal religious order. Friars can also be priests.

irrigation (eer-ih-GAY-shun) Supplying with water.

livestock (LYV-stahk) Farm animals kept for use or profit.

Mass (MAS) A Christian religious ceremony.

missionary (MIH-shuh-nayr-ee) A person who teaches his or her religion to people with different beliefs.

neophyte (NEE-uh-fyt) The name for an American Indian once he or she was baptized into the Christian faith.

New Spain (NOO SPAYN) The area where the Spanish colonists had their capital in North America and that would later become Mexico.

quadrangle (KWAH-drayn-gul) The square at the center of a mission that is surrounded by four buildings.

secularization (seh-kyoo-luh-rih-ZAY-shun) When a person or place is made to be nonreligious.

tule (TOO-lee) Tightly woven reeds used by American Indians to help build their homes.

viceroy (VYS-roy) The governor of a place who rules as a representative of the king.

villages (VIH-lih-jiz) Original communities where American Indians lived before the arrival of the Spanish, non-Christian, or nonmission, Indians continued to live in these villages.

Pronunciation Guide

atole (ah-TOH-lay)

El Camino Real (EL kah-MEE-noh RAY-al)

fray (FRAY)

lavandería (lah-ban-deh-REE-ah)

monjerío (mohn-hay-REE-oh)

pozole (poh-SOH-lay)

pozolero (poh-soh-LAIR-oh)

pueblos (PWAY-blohz)

rancherías (rahn-cheh-REE-ahs)

siesta (see-EHS-tah)

temescal (TEH-mes-cal)

tomol (TOH-mul)

Resources

To learn more about the missions of California, check out these books and Web sites:

Books

Fraser, Mary Ann. *A Mission for the People: The Story of La Purísima.* New York, NY: Henry Holt, 1997.

Van Steenwyk, Elizabeth. *The California Missions.* New York, NY: Franklin Watts, 1995.

Young, Stanley. *The Missions of California.* San Francisco, CA: Chronicle Books, 1998.

Web Sites
Due to the changing nature of Internet links, PowerKids Press has developed an online list of Web sites related to the subject of this book. This site is updated regularly. Please use this link to access the list: www.powerkidslinks.com/moca/mlapucon/

Index